S O H O

S O H O

A PICTURE PORTRAIT BY CARL GLASSMAN

UNIVERSE BOOKS
New York

for April

Book designed by
Burt Kleeger

Published in the United States of America in 1985
by Universe Books
381 Park Avenue South, New York, N.Y. 10016

Copyright © 1985 by Carl Glassman

Introduction copyright © 1985 by John Leonard

85 86 87 88 89 / 10 9 8 7 6 5 4 3 2 1

Printed in the United States of America

Library of Congress Cataloging-in-Publication Data

Glassman, Carl.
    Soho, a photographic portrait.

    1. SoHo (New York, N.Y.) – Description – Views.
2. New York (N.Y.) – Description – 1981–   –Views.
I. Title.
F128.68.S64G53   1985   974.7'1   85-8507
ISBN 0-87663-566-4

INTRODUCTION

Back in the Pleistocene epoch, when Eisenhower was president and I was a cabbage child in a fatigue jacket trying to be either sincere or authentic, there was this room I rented, for nine dollars a week, at the corner of MacDougal and Bleecker, near free opera and expensive coffee, very Beat. Houston was not my street; I didn't even know how to pronounce it. On my map, it was the margin of the heart of darkness. After nine o'clock at night, South of Houston was ghost time and ghost place in the area now known as SoHo, cast iron and Indians and sewing machines, like a New England mill town, some other century, anterior to Edison and publicity.

In the Sixties, when everybody was being sincere and authentic, an artist friend of mine specialized, on Broome Street, in the creation of thermoplastic eggs. Those eggs (each one three times the size of a man) were trying to find a way to copulate — or so they were meant to appear. I used to visit them by freight elevator, feeling diminished. My friend, the mother of those eggs, was illegal. You were not allowed to live in those big open spaces left empty by manufacturers who had moved to New Jersey and elsewhere. There were no cabs to get you out of all this industrial history. It was cold in the sweat shop.

Then John V. Lindsay decided that artists were citizens, too, and those Indians, making eggs and whatever else, deserved a

lot of light and space. He legalized the lofts. I was busy at the time, uptown, reading books for a living, and it never occurred to me to wonder whether to declare yourself an artist—to register or enlist, by way of qualifying for light and space—was a good idea or a bad joke: Hereby and therefore I pledge that I am sincere and authentic and deserve a zoning variance.

I went to the SoHo of Carl Glassman's photographs. We are no longer talking about the heart of darkness. There are nearly a hundred galleries in the neighborhood; five different ones in a single building, with track lighting. The heart of darkness has been boutiqued. The Indians hang out at Dimitri's, drinking iced capuccino. You can buy a pencil that's bigger than your average Aztec. Everybody wears a T-shirt, advertising himself or a service or a disease: DEATH BEFORE MELLOW. It's zoo time, and the animals demand to be snapshot.

One thinks, too, of the circus, and its outrageous spectacles. The circus has come to town, and the out-of-towners have come to the circus. The eye reels and so does the mind, in whirligig; marble and wood and stained glass and plexiglass and antique lace; campaign posters and rock video and xerography and computerized dimming systems; animal heads on human figures and peopleless landscapes, after some apocalyptic scourge, and peopleless abstractions, a sullen mystique—a kind of fretting of raw edges with any old knife as if to

torture texture and bend the color band. And here at the circus are the tourists—families, students, louts, self-packagers in search of a slogan or a jingle, the glib and the dumbfounded and those who are hungry for light and those just hoping to be dazzled into sentience. And they are all standing around dressed up like so many crayons, as if to scribble themselves, as if, like children at the circus, they needed to be told when to turn on their flashlights, their magic dancing lanterns. "Aesthetics is for the artist," said Barnett Newman, "what ornithology is for the birds."

Something odd has happened to art. It has been zoned. It wants to subvert—a savage eye, a scorpion chastisement—but it has been gentrified, rather too polite pinned to its white walls, promulgated in its own newspapers (free of charge) like *Artspeak* and *The New Common Good*. Art is licensed. It walks around its ten square blocks on a leash of gaudy ribbon. It ingratiates and preens.

And there isn't enough really dangerous art, which threatens and alters our perception. We semaphore with credit cards, as art runs away, ever fugitive; Castelli can't catch it. But Glassman does, because he is on the streets instead of lofty. SoHo people advertise themselves, as if they knew that the wheeler-dealers in loft speculation would never get it right; they publicize and proclaim, with blue palm prints and punk haircuts, in leather and neon; they are self-framing cat people, mimes, wish fulfillments, robots, Isadora Duncans, toys, outdoor sculpture. They insist: I am special and vivid and not a ghost, nor acrylic, nor tempera.

It is as if Glassman were saying, on behalf of the people he photographs: We are our own art, a performing self; we have come here to be seen. And Glassman sees them: innocent, cunning, striking attitudes like matches, "found," parodied, gargoyled, hologrammed. His camera is shrewd and affectionate and comical in this art zone. He assists in the inventing of selves, the merchandizing of dreamy variations, that the lofts are too busy to. His is a splendid notice.

How strange: In these pictures, we tour ourselves. We would be lost, in SoHo, among competing flamboyances, without such a camera eye. Glassman isolates the idea of ourself we chose to declare south of the border, in Indian territory. We can't, anymore, in SoHo, be alone. We can, in these photographs, recognize the unseen self, which is what art is about, and SoHo, charging three-fifty and five bucks a drink at the Spring Street Bar, has forgotten. Once upon a time it was a magic hunting ground, and then an industrial waste without light after dark, and now it is a circus where the tourists come, looking again for the Indians, the savage yawp.

John Leonard

THOMAS BACHER

381 West Broadway.

**Daisy Youngblood show at
Barbara Gladstone Gallery.**

Curious visitors gather on West Broadway.

Nikki Young, a saleswoman at the clothing store Trash and Vaudeville.

"We get a lot of tourists that don't buy and just look. They come in and gawk at us and laugh. It makes me feel like I'm in a cage in a way."

Nikki Young

The Wine Bar.

On the corner of Spring Street and
West Broadway.

**Horace Post. His sign reads:
"BADLY CRIPPLED BROKE AGE 71."**

"I can make very good money here—about two dollars an hour. The people are very generous and friendly, and they're very well-versed and literate, too. That's something you don't find everywhere."

Horace Post

Dianne Benson, owner of the SoHo clothing stores Dianne B. and Comme Des Garcons.

"We opened in SoHo in 1982 with much bigger results than I ever expected. It was very exciting. We were the only game in town for interesting, expensive clothes. One year later, there were millions of stores selling the same sort of clothes we do, but the month-later cheap version. This glut really shook up our clientele and we experienced a slump that was so depressing. Now we're beginning to find our own again and things are feeling perkier."

Dianne Benson

**Artist Keith Haring draws on the shirt
of an admirer.**

Artist selling hand-painted T-shirts.

Ivan Karp, whose O.K. Harris Gallery was the first ground-level gallery in SoHo.

"To be an art dealer, you don't have to take a test. It's not like civil service. You have a little cash or a supporter, four clean walls, and you put stuff on them and say, 'This is what art should be today.' I poke around the neighborhood and look in the galleries. I've never seen such trash in my life as I have in the last two years. This is the darkest moment. There's incredible talent around, too. Absolutely ripe, ready, first-class artists and nothing happens to them. It's a sad story."

Ivan Karp

Wigmaker Carrie Tuke and painter Peter White in their Broadway loft.

"It's difficult to live in a working situation. I get paint in my hair and he gets hair in his paint. Sometimes you just want to get away from it."

Carrie Tuke

**Checking hair tint outside of Girl Loves Boy,
a Thompson Street salon.**

**Fia on the phone. Trash and
Vaudeville boutique.**

Dress designer and manufacturer Lucille Chayt. Dresses at her Broome Street store sell for $300 to $1,400.

"I was waiting to open my store in SoHo, but it wasn't until recently that stores opened with prices that are compatible with my prices. It's taken a long time for it to go in that direction, but now it's going crazy in that direction."

Lucille Chayt

Julio and Ica, of Susanne Bartsch boutique.

"If you're uptown dressed like this, people think you're a freak or you're weird. Down here, everyone's an individual, and that's the point. Why do you want to walk around looking like everybody else? We're all completely different. Even if we strip off our clothes, we're completely different."

Julio

Evening shoppers.

Opening. Tony Shafrazi Gallery.

Vigdor Ziskind, co-owner of ABC Wiping Materials Co., on Greene Street.

"SoHo? It's a new style of craziness. Crazy stores looking for crazy people. . . . For some people it's good, for others, they have to lose their business. A lot of old people just gave up. There used to be over sixty rag businesses around here. Now there are five or six."

Vigdor Ziskind

Artist Al Held in his loft that overlooks West Broadway. Held has lived there since 1968.

"If I'm idly looking outside while I'm work-ing, it's not particularly good to see the com-merce on the street. It diverts the mind. And it's not amusing to be sitting here on Saturday afternoon and see a guy walking level with your window, doing a tight-rope act. SoHo is a three-ring circus out there. If I weren't old and fat I would have picked up and left."

Al Held

**A mime performs on West Broadway and
Prince Street.**

Don Robertus waits on a customer at the boutique Chaserie.

"The customers down here have much more individuality. They're not buying a designer's name. They all have a mind of their own or they come to me and they get a style of their own."

Don Robertus

Outside the Cupping Room Cafe.

Break dancers.

**Men shucking oysters at the opening
of the clothing store In-Wear.**

Gallery owners Mary Boone and Leo Castelli.

"I never even think about SoHo. The art world is not so geographically oriented, certainly not on such a small, petty level. I look at SoHo as a subset of a very huge world that includes London, Paris, Hamburg, Cologne, Berlin, and Tokyo. This is just a small part of it."

Mary Boone

René, an artist who exhibits in his own small gallery on Wooster Street, restores his 10-foot by 50-foot mural on Broome Street and West Broadway. The "I Am The Best Artist" painting is frequently defaced.

"The art establishment wouldn't even acknowledge that I existed. So I decided it was up to me to make myself known. . . . If you want to advertise something, you have to create an image, so I came up with "I Am The Best Artist." Now I can safely claim that everybody knows about me, because if you have not seen that sign, you have nothing to do with art or you've never been to SoHo. Of course, people write on it and say it sucks. But I thrive on that. It's a reaction. I just don't want you to ignore me."

René

Raoul's Restaurant.

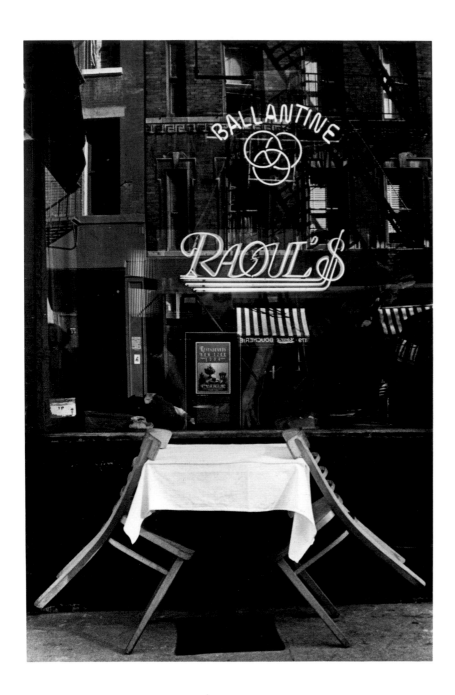

Jewelry sellers on Prince Street.

135 Prince Street.

Outside of Ken and Bob's Broome Street Bar.

Police Officer Robert Schidowski outside Lulu's on West Broadway.

"SoHo is the fun place to be on the weekends. Everything else in the precinct is quiet."

Officer Robert Schidowski

Greene Street near Canal.

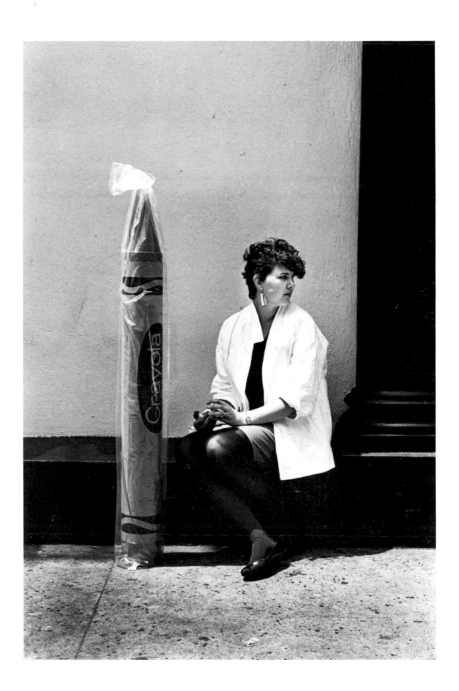

Bob and Meryl Gold and daughter Morgan, from Hartsdale, N.Y., visit SoHo once or twice a month.

"We live in Westchester, but I don't like to look like a Westchesterite. Everyone looks the same there. It's a great, free feeling to be in SoHo. It has that arty-type atmosphere. I feel more at home with my hair the way it is and everything."

Meryl Gold

SoHo artist Barbara Zweig, with daughter Lauren, at demonstration against New York Loft Board, which artists say is biased toward landlords and is attempting to "regulate moderate-income artists out of existence."

"I've lived in SoHo since 1969. It was really better back then. You knew everybody. Your next-door neighbor was an artist. We didn't feel that we were competing with the boutiques and the whole uptown rat race. Now SoHo is more of a supermarket than a cultural center and we feel like we're being kicked out of the neighborhood. Where are the artists going? That's what I want to know."

Barbara Zweig

**Hollywood Legend, a clothing store
on Spring Street.**

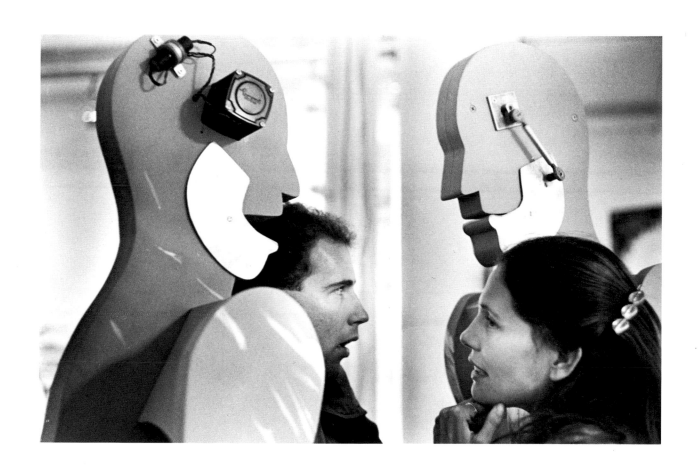

Jon Borofsky show. Paula Cooper Gallery.

Performance artist Kim Jones at Germans Van Eck Gallery.

"If I took my stuff to the Bowery or Brooklyn, it would be like pissing in the ocean. I'd just be this funny thing that's happening out there. But in SoHo, artists and people interested in art see me. I just take the subway, walk in, and I have a show for a day."

Kim Jones

"Pin Screen" demonstration on West Broadway.

**Artist Noël Mapstead at opening at
Manhattan Art.**

"I don't think many artists get shows by taking
slides around to the galleries. Going to openings and meeting people is the only way to be
successful. Last year, I went to about 1,200
openings and picked up 30 shows — and I never
asked for one of them. Now that I know the
gallery scene inside and out I'm more selec-
tive. I only go to three or four openings a
night instead of fifteen.

Noël Mapstead

Ellie Reichler, 14, in the Wooster Street loft where she lives with her father, Mel, and brother, Jesse.

"Of the twenty or twenty-five couples I've known in SoHo over the last ten years, two—maybe three—have stayed together. It's a disaster zone for marriage."

Mel Reichler

"I think I have a lot more guts than kids who grow up in other places. I'm not afraid to try new things. But I don't have a goal in life—yet. A lot of kids in SoHo don't know where they're headed."

Ellie Reichler

Cat and woman on West Broadway.

Two dogs on West Broadway.

Donald Heller playes the hurdy gurdy, a medieval instrument, on West Broadway.

"My music is art on a human scale in the midst of all the hype of the clothes and visual art that's on sale in SoHo. You can give a quarter or a dollar or whatever you want. Take it or leave it, nobody's manipulating your tastes or desires."

Donald Heller

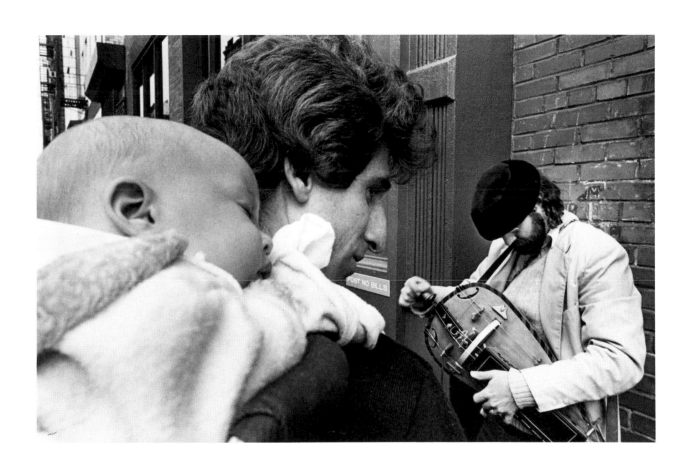

Ron, Justine, David, and "Holly Golightly."

"We're going to be famous one day and ride around in a limo. So we come here now and let everyone see us. . . get it while you can."

"Holly Golightly"

The jewelry store Artwear.

Parachute, a clothing store on Wooster Street.

Laurie Mallet in her Prince Street loft.

"When my husband and I moved into this loft we were only two. Now I have two kids and a nanny. Even though this is a huge space, it's not planned for children. I have this feeling of non-privacy always."

Laurie Mallet

Bill Reichenbach is a mechanic for the R.K. Bakery, which used to be on Prince Street in SoHo. He began his gallery of found-art objects outside the bakery in 1979. None of the work is for sale.

"When I started my gallery, it was going to be a gag for a couple of weeks. But I got a very favorable response from most of the people who'd stop and look. Some of them tell me that this is better than anything they've seen in SoHo. One guy offered me $500 for my favorite piece, which is a chunk of cast-iron boiler that I painted two stripes on and mounted. This tends to turn your head, but on the other hand I realize that most of the people are no more of an authority on art than I am."

Bill Reichenbach

Rizzoli International Bookstore.

Saturday afternoon on West Broadway.

Carmella Fazio (left) and Mary Farango in front of the Thompson Street apartment building where the two women were born. (Carmella still lives there. Mary lives down the block.) Escalating rents on Thompson Street, part of an Italian-American neighborhood since the turn of the century, have forced most of the stores catering to local residents to close their doors. Boutiques have taken their places.

"There used to be six grocery stores on this block. Now there's only one. Next door was a grocery even when I was a little girl. It's terrible what's happened to these businesses. It's like a ghost town — like the Germans went through. Zoom! There's nobody on the goddamn block anymore."

Mary Farango

"It's all out-of-towner people going in the new stores. But you don't see them doing that much business. I don't know how they make it."

Carmella Fazio

Bruce Nauman show. Sperone Westwater Gallery.

Opening. Stellweg Gallery.

Thompson Street park.

Carl Glassman's photographs have been exhibited in museums and galleries in the United States as well as in England, Israel, China, and Japan. Exhibitions of photographs from this book were shown in 1985 at O.K. Harris Gallery in New York and Photographers' Gallery in London. His work has been published in The New York Times, Newsweek, Camera Arts, American Photographer, Natural History, and many other publications in the United States and Europe. He has also worked as a writer and is the author of two books and numerous magazine articles.

Glassman, a native of Oklahoma City, lives in New York City and teaches photojournalism at New York University.